# RaceBrave

# RaceBrave

Karsonya Wise Whitehead

Apprentice House
Loyola University Maryland
Baltimore, Maryland

First Edition

Printed in the United States of America

Hardcover ISBN: 978-1-62720-117-9
Paperback ISBN: 978-1-62720-118-6
E-book ISBN: 978-1-62720-119-3

Design by Apprentice House
Editorial Assistant: Karl Dehmelt
Cover by Calvin Coleman
Author Photo by Christopher Singlemann

Published by Apprentice House

Apprentice House
Loyola University Maryland
4501 N. Charles Street
Baltimore, MD 21210
410.617.5265 • 410.617.2198 (fax)
www.ApprenticeHouse.com
info@ApprenticeHouse.com

# Contents

## Section III

for my mother
...who gave me wings, paper, and a pen
and then set me free

for mercedes (my sweet daughter)
...for patiently teaching me how to be your Momma Kaye

for "Auntie" Maya Angelou
...who in 1999 told me, with a smile,
"Keep writing baby, the world needs your words."

# Acknowledgements

*Men go abroad to wonder at the heights of mountains,*
*at the huge waves of the sea,*
*at the long courses of the rivers,*
*at the vast compass of the ocean,*
*at the circular motions of the stars,*
*and they pass by themselves without wondering.*
— *St. Augustine*

Every time I start on a new book project, I spend some time thinking about what St. Augustine once said, as it perfectly sums up the life I carved out for myself as a writer and a speaker. I spend hours wandering into myself, obsessing over every word and comma and period. I get into bed every night with my computer, stacks of papers, and a box of pencils. I wake up every morning and greet my written words before I greet my family. I stare in awe and wonder as the book begins to get written, one line at a time, one page at a time. And, while all of this is happening, my family quietly tries to work itself around my schedule. I think that they have become accustomed to losing me when I am trying to finish a book. I know that I am only able to do the work that I do because my husband and my children provide the wind that I need to soar. They are the ones who are charged with the great responsibility of having to nurture a writer, having to mother a speaker, and having to love a poet. I stand taller because they have allowed me to stand on their shoulders. They have also allowed me the space to return back to them, empty, after I have poured out everything I have either into a book or into an audience. They see me and all of my faults and love me anyway. To my little ones: Mercedes Alexandria, Kofi Elijah, and Amir Elisha: thank you for choosing me. Everyday you find small ways to bring me such joy and happiness. You make me proud to call myself your mother. To my life partner, my best friend, and to the one who makes me feel safe whenever he is around, Johnnie Whitehead—thank you for telling me over and over again all the reasons why you love me.

Outside of my family, there are others who have loved and supported, challenged and pushed me along the way: my extended family (my parents, Carson and Bonnie, my siblings Labonnie, Robin, Carson II, Verneal, Shanell, Terrell and Tiarra, and Eric; and, Harriet and Monica Kelly), thank you for always being there to lend support, to provide guidance, and to gently push me back in the right direction; to the Family Fun Night crew (O'Neal and Lajuana Johnson, Best and Stephanie Davis, Stephen and Kenya Davol, Dwayne and Jillian Garner, and Jose and Judy Jiminez), I am looking forward to the day when all of our kids are in (or have graduated from) college and we can sit down and laugh and cry about how we made it over; to the Happy Hairstons (Thom and Olivia, Dorna, Vince and Yvette, Jeffrey and Tody), thank you for the sisterly love and support; to my academic support team (La Vonne Neal, Sylvia Cyrus, Regina Lewis, Alicia Moore, Conra Gist, Martha Wharton, and Kelly Cross), thank you for the never ending support and for the encouragement; and, finally, thank you to Abigail Jerome, who always found a way to just be there for us. None of this would be possible without my editor, Kevin Atticks, who takes my dreams and helps me turn them into books.

And since some of these poems are over twenty years old, I must go back and thank folks who told me way back then that I was a poet and that my work had value: Kenny Carroll, DJ Renegade, Matty Rochester, Rana Walker, Tschaka Walker, Beverly Mathis, Clive and Yvette Davis, Eric Wray, Baraka Smith, Les King, Tawanda Beale, Guy Sims, both my line sisters (from the 18 Disorderlies!) and my sorority sisters of Delta Sigma Theta (Zeta Omega Chapter), Stacey Davis, Edgar Mitchell (gone way too soon), and Eric Webb.

Finally, in this wonderful age of social media—and the ease in which we move in and out of each other's lives, I must also thank my Facebook friends for reading my works in progress and for cheering me along the way; with special mentions to my fellow alum from William McKinley High School; Lincoln University, PA; and, the University of Notre Dame; and, to all of my sista' scholars who meet me every year on the hallowed academic grounds of either the National Women's Studies Association (NWSA) or the Association for the Study of African American Life and History (ASALH) to break bread, to share stories, to laugh and to cry, so that we can get built up and be ready to throw our backs against the wind once more.

## the beginning...

I have been writing poetry for as long as I can remember. It is the power of the pen on paper that has sustained me and has kept me. It is the one place that I consider to be my familiar, where I am most at home and where I do not feel like I am alone. I wrote my first poem when I was 12 years old. I remember that I was sitting in my homeroom class and I was sweating, because it was so hot. My teacher had already moved me from my seat beside the window, complaining that I spent too much time staring out it. I used to stare out of it and try to imagine what life was like on the other side of it. I felt like I was living life from inside of a wall. I used to doodle in my notebooks, writing my name on line after line. And then I wrote this:

## heed the call: i know who i am

I am karsonyaeugeniawise
my name is too big for my mouth
my mother says I will grow in to it

I am a student a prisoner a daughter

I have no friends
they say I cant be trusted
to keep secrets
that arent my own

I look at them and try to imagine my way
into their world
I will not be silent

even if no one is listening

I am not a murderer
(I do not count the lightening bugs I suffocated
the roaches I stepped on
or the bugs that I burned with my microscope)
But, I have confessed my sins
And now my hands are clean

I know who I am
neither complicated nor complex
and everyday I take stock all over again

I am not really poor
(there are girls you like who are poorer)
or really ugly
(there are girls you like who are uglier)
or really mean
(there are girls you like who are meaner)
but I am me and that should be enough

is it wrong to want to be liked by those who hate me
those who laugh at me when I walk by
or who wont make room for me at the table

I think that I should change my name
start all over and get it right this time

I read this poem today and my heart aches for the person I
used to be. I remember what it was like to feel isolated, and to
feel alone. Poetry in so many ways saved my life. On the days
when I felt that I had reached the end of who I was, I would go
back and read my work and tell myself that I still had more to say,
more to share, and more to give to the world, even if they were

not smart enough to realize it. I did not know what to do with my work (how I wish my parents knew how to parent a writer) so I just stockpiled them, similar to the way rodents stockpile trash or squirrels stockpile nuts. I wrote on everything I could find, on paper, on napkins, on the walls, on my arms. I had to get the words out because this is how I reminded myself that I was still here even when I felt like I was disappearing.

I started performing poetry when I was in college. I would sign up for slam poetry contests, honing my voice and sharpening my sword. It was on the stage (a place that I had been on for years as I grew up in a black church where my father often had me recite scriptures on Sunday mornings) where I finally found myself exactly where I wanted to be. Sharing my poetry, this piece of myself, felt like my small act of attrition, an individual baptism that cleansed me and prepared me to go back out into the world. The lines between the classroom, my heart, and my life were blurred, as everything found its way into my work. The first poem I ever performed was "intentional freedom: a guide book." I was in Washington, DC, at a restaurant in Adams Morgan, and the poetry slam was held right before Arrested Development was scheduled to perform. I won the slam that night and when I left the stage, the lead singer told me that I should publish it and give it to every enlightened brother that I knew for mediation and prayer:

## intentional freedom: a guide book

Over kisses and empty promises
You told me that you wanted to love me
But couldnt get past my independence
Couldnt get over my need to be on top
Couldnt figure out a way to make me submit

You said you wanted to be my king
and lead me to the promise land
but you couldnt accept my unbowed head
my unbent knee my unwrapped hair

you said you wanted to love me
you just needed me to let you
you –you said– were frustrated
because I wouldnt cook
didnt ask about your day
never tried to grab your hand
I didnt long for you

You needed me to act like a wummon
And let you love me, finally and completely
And in frustration, one day, you asked me how…

1. start by taking your foot off of my throat
(you cannot silence my tongue/wummon and strong/thick and
all mine)

2. then get your hands out of my uterus
(you cannot own or control that which belongs only to me)

and when you bow your head to pray

3. remove yourself from my mouth
(the road to my heart will not be built at the altar of the weapon
that you wield)

I remember this poem because it was the first one I felt I could
not share with my parents. My boyfriend at the time, never heard
this poem (he was not there that night) and I believe that I only
performed it once (the version I performed was much different,

much racier, than the version I wrote). This was not for him as he never tried to control me, never got frustrated about loving me, never demanded or asked for my submission. But I wrote it anyway and it came from somewhere within me. My poems (like my children) are not my own, sometimes they come through me and I just bear witness to the story.

My first chapbook was *red zinger lov/starved blues: notes of a wummon/child* and it sold exactly 100 copies (they were numbered). I used to travel around with them in my bag and like every other starving poet, I would pull them out and try to sell them on the spot. I was young then and the world through a poet's eye seemed bleak. I was depressed all of the time and was absolutely convinced that the racism and sexism that was rampant in this country, was going to kill me before I turned 30. I never thought I would grow old, never thought I would get married, or have children, or get gray hair. But I did and over time, my poetry gave way to essays, my short stories gave way to academic papers, my depression gave way to enjoying the moments of extraordinary joy that just come from still being here. I have spent years struggling in the darkness, thinking about what it means to be brave, to be a fighter. I have spent years trying to remember what my voice sounded like. I have spent hours trying to trust myself enough to be as honest on the page today as I was when I first began. I have stepped out into darkness, time and time again, and without fail, there has always been something very strong for me to stand on or I have been taught how to fly.

I started writing *RaceBrave* on July 7, 2014, on the day when Eric Garner was murdered. It was on that day, two years after the murder of Trayvon Martin and after coming through Ferguson being repeated throughout the country, that I realized that I too could no longer breathe. I could no longer swallow the lies. I had to find a way to be RaceBrave and to give a voice to my pain.

Some of the poems are brand new (having been written from 7.17.14 to 7.17.15); a few were written twenty years ago and I have just found the courage to have them meet me on the public page (because part of being RaceBrave means you have the courage to finally speak your truth); and, a few have found their way in various iterations into other publications. *RaceBrave* incudes all of this along with diary entries, excerpts from speeches, and some of my favorite family stories. It has been a long road but I have finally come back to the poet I used to be.

Karsonya Wise Whitehead
*Baltimore, MD*

# Section I

your silence will not protect you

## dreaming

to my Nana who came to me in a dream
with a song of freedom and a shout of praise
and though she died blind
she could see me and called me by her childhood name
she said run the race  she said don't stop  she said be brave
and she kept saying it and saying it
until the words began to blend together
and all I heard was racebrave racebrave racebrave

## hearing

to the young sister who I met in Freddie Grey's neighborhood
wearing a #BlackLivesMatter t-shirt
who when it was time to march grabbed my hand
squeezed it and said be brave, pass it on
me: confused, unsure just for a moment
be brave? I said, pass it on?
yes, sister, be brave and then pass it on.

## doing

to Claudia Rankine
who spoke at Loyola one cold night in January
who in a moment of unguarded joy
told us (like she had been told)

to be race brave  to be courageous
and what I heard but she didn't actually say was
to just be

## modeling

to my sons who have spent their lives
gaining wisdom while growing up and getting stronger
who learned what it meant to be courageous
in the face of incredible fear
who taught me that racebrave was a call to action
that racebrave was a moment to change
that racebrave, simply put,
meant having the words to say
and having the courage to say them

## singing

to the activist I want to be
and to the mother that I try to be
to the scholar who makes me work
and to the writer who makes me work harder
to the daughter and to the sister
to the wife and to the friend
all of these equal parts that make up who I am
it took me all of my life
but I am finally RaceBrave
and I will sing that and my #BlackLivesMatter song
until the whole world hears

# today, my heart stopped

7.17.14 Eric Garner
he said, I cant breathe.
I cant breathe. I cant breathe.
I Cant Breathe.  ICantBreatheICantBreathe.
ICantBreatheICantBreatheICantBreatheICantBreathe.
I. Cant. Breathe.
they said, And you will never breathe again.

7.17.14 again
today, my heart stopped as
hoodies, skittles, iced tea
hands up, don't shoot
loud rap music in parked cars
babies asleep on couches
mistaken homes, doors kicked in
mistaken identities, because we all look alike
have given way
to illegal choke holds
to being killed
for wanting to be left alone
for asking questions and demanding answers
for being frustrated
for not going silently into their night
for wanting to  breathe
and for daring to demand these simple things outLoud

# what happens when the lights go out

And now like Ferguson like New York like South Carolina
Baltimore has become some type of place
where some cops white or black or brown
male or female
masquerade as judge jury executioner
where we find ourselves with questions
and no answers
in mourning but without tears
in jungles concrete no glass
in prisons controlled guarded no bars
in hell our sins judged by sinners
dripping blood from their teeth
tearing our hearts straight out of our chest.

We must remember
that only the wicked see black skin as a sign of guilt
mistake loaded guns for tasers
running as an act of confession
wallets for loaded weapons
see toy guns as real
they never hear our shouts for help as real
they cant believe that we cant breathe
that we want to be free
that we want to grow up.

They cant accept that we belong here  too
that it is our blood that runs thick with the same soil
that we use to grow our organic food
our pain being used to feed a nation  again

our young brothers and sisters
now ageless and faceless
martyrs really
did not die did not pass away they are not lost
they were killed murdered shot choked
they are not lost
we know exactly where they are.

# dreaming outLoud

Friday, January 8, 2016 (Baltimore City)

**4:30p** I am sitting in a coffee shop on a cold, wet, and rainy day reading the City Paper Vol. 40 No. 1. They profiled the 344 people that were killed last year in Baltimore City. They. Said. Their. Names. They made them real to us. They gave us their stories, provided us with some background, the times of their deaths, and they gave a running tally so we could see how the city went from the first death on Saturday, January 3 12:07 a.m. (Leon Flemming) to the last one on Thursday, December 31 8:15 p.m. (Jameel Woodward). I want to work for a paper that makes a decision to make this number mean something. I sat there and said each name and read each story out loud to my youngest son. We must be the ones that remember them. We must find solutions to stop this leaky valve. We must be the ones to change this reality. We must be the ones that we have been waiting for.

**5:30p** I am experiencing a moment of cognitive dissonance as I sit in a fancy shamancy coffee shop –one of only two black people here– reading the names and stories of all of these black people (mostly men and boys) who were killed in this city last year. I look around and wonder if I am the only person who feels like the air is being sucked out of the room, one name at a time, one story at a time, one breath at a time. I now understand why I wake up angry and ready to fight every single day and go to bed every night praying and breathing a sigh of relief. I now understand why I really believe that I am suffering from PTPRD (post-traumatic post-racial disorder). According to the City Paper, "If you are a young black man in Baltimore, you are 30 times more likely to die on the streets here than if you had grown up elsewhere in the US."

I am raising two black boys with my black husband in Baltimore City and every day they leave the house, I realize, with a sigh/with a deep rooted moan/with tears in my eyes, that I could be Tamir's mother, I could be Trayvon's mother, I could be Jordan's mother, I could be Walter's wife, I could be Eric's wife…I could be that person. I reach over to my son, sitting next to me, holding a book in one hand and his phone in the other, and I touch him –just to remind myself that he is still here, he is safe, and he is still (if only for a moment) close enough for me to jump in front of him if something happens.

**5:45p** I cannot breathe. I cannot see. I cannot stop shaking. Page 24 Name #288 – this is the moment when everything stops for me. I stopped reading, I stopped drinking my coffee, I stopped reading names in my casual yet concerned voice and I get up and leave the coffee shop because I cannot stop crying. –Darryl WHITEHEAD, #288, was shot in the head and died at 3:44 p.m. on Wednesday, November 4. My son follows me out of the coffee shop; he grabs my hand and wants to know if Darryl could have been related to us. "Yes," I said, as I slowly drag my tired, bone-weary spirit to my car – "he could have been one of us." I sit in the car, lay my head down on the steering wheel and took a long deep breath – Darryl Whitehead could have been my son, he could have been my cousin. He is, even though I do not know him, one of us. I want to know his story. I want to meet his family. I want to say his name and remember it like he was my own.

**8:45p** My sons are home. They are in the basement, playing with their X-Box, laughing about their day. They are home, waiting for dinner and wondering aloud if they will be able to stay up late and get dessert. They are home and their coats and shoes, and books and gloves are strewn about the house. They are home and they are complaining about whose job it is to take out the dog and make his dinner. They are home and they do not have a care in the world. Not at this moment. My boys are home and Darryl Whitehead is not. I step outside onto my back porch and I say his name again and again, in the hope that it will be picked up by the wind and that his family –somewhere here in Baltimore– will feel it and know that I am in mourning, too.

# black mommy activism p1

for ten days without fail
you marched for freddie grey
you marched for justice
you marched and dreamed of a better world
in search of a better tomorrow
away from all of our yesterdays

you marched because you wanted to be free
having spent your life listening for the whispers of freedom
you thought you were on your way to free/dom
and that the road went straight through east baltimore
straight through freddie grey's block
straight through his home
straight through his life

and so you marched
never having marched before
never having struggled before
never having ... before

you marched and marched
you complained while marching
you cried out while marching
and then, you found yourself while marching.

I marched too
but I simply marched for you.

## courage means being able to bless yourself
### (for amir)

you were only four
when I discovered who you were

that you were who I had been waiting for

I had been waiting for a teacher
for a guide, for a *raboni*
for someone to show me the way

I expected you to be older
I expected you to be grayer
I expected you to be able to carry me
instead; like Mary, I carried you
for nine months and beyond
I sustained you; nutrients and all

you were my second born, a baby really

and on that day you were playing in your room by yourself
having just learned how to amuse yourself,
if only for a moment,
you were quiet intense focused

and then you sneezed and then you yelled,
"God bless you, Amir"
I was confused and amused all at once
and I called you down because I had to know

you said,
"sometimes when you are by yourself, you gotta bless yourself."

"you do," I said, "you do"
I wrote it on a sign and put it up on my wall
and for a long time, every time I cried
waiting for answers that never came
I would simply say, "God bless you," and then I added my name

courage is being able to bless yourself
when no one else can see your genius
when they doubt you or ignore you
when they try to silence and
try to break you

courage, i have found, is being able to bless yourself
sometimes when you are by yourself you gotta be bold enough
be courageous enough be racebrave enough
to bless yourself

my teacher, who knew I needed answers
and guidance and direction, taught me this

# speaking with my father's tongue

I speak as one who has been raised right
who knows the difference between right and wrong
being brave enough to name my demons
one by one.

I am the daughter of folks who made it out
who cloaked themselves in success
while protecting us from racism
while protecting us from ourselves.

I speak as a voice of inherited reason and tried wisdom
speaking with my father's tongue
native-born jim crow boy
who learned how to hate white skin
while learning the rules of the south,

who remembers what life was like before the internet,
colored television,
men on the moon, cellphones, but not racism.
He has never known a world with out racism.

He remembers Jim Crow, little Rock Nine, Bull O'Conner,
and dogs named nigger
and when some folks said that they would rather blow up a
church
than allow black people to worship their God in peace.
He remembers life before Brown
and nights of potluck and potpourri and rent parties
and raised rent.

He remembers when SNCC reminded us;
the Nation of Islam schooled us; the Black Panthers protected
us; and, the government tracked us.
He remembers how the air was different with Martin, with
Malcolm, and with Medgar…

He is a long-memoried person.
I am a quilt, stitched together by his life experiences
whose earliest memory of love

involves laying across his neck watching television
when I was two.

I don't remember what we talked about,
what I was wearing,
or what day it was,
I just remember that there was a lot of love and laughter
and hugs and kisses.

Baby girls should have daddies who make them feel loved
who remind them never to forget,
who share their memories and experiences;
knowing the story of every scar, the deep roots where pain exists
who remembers them before
before they found themselves
before they loved themselves
before they turned themselves into themselves.

## songs in a key called baltimore

I would like to write a song about peace/about reconciliation/ about a city coming back together and working for the common good.

I would like to write that #BlackLivesMatter and point to the ways in which this simple concept/screamed and shouted, cried over and prayed about/has transformed the city and altered our space.

I would like to teach my sons about peace in a city while raising them in a city where peace has never been the norm/where peace is not taught on the playground/not practiced in the school/not modeled on the street corner.

I try and hide my frustration because in the aftermath of an Uprising/a time where people named their pain/life has settled back down to the familiar to a time where black bodies are endangered, black life is criminalized, and black spaces exist on the edges of both the city and our minds.

I am not old enough to remember life before *Brown v Board*, when black and white spaces were clearly marked.

I suspect (though) that it was not much different than it is now in places around Baltimore and places across America where the crime of breathing while black is still punishable by death.

My heart always skips a beat when a cop's car is behind me while I am driving at night/and though my sons are not old enough to drive, I am already frightened/concerned/angry/frustrated as I think about the day when they will be stopped for the crime of driving while black.

There are days when being black in America overwhelms me and makes me want to spend the day in bed/and times when being the black mother of black boys in Baltimore City makes me wish I had enough money to move them somewhere where I could keep them safe.

Safe from them—the ones who see their lives as expendable and unnecessary/and safe from us—those who look at them without realizing that they are mirrors that simply reflect all of who we are supposed to be.

I often think about slavery and how different life was when you could see the hand that held the chain that was attached to the ball that was tied to your ankle.

We come from a people who experienced this daily and still chose to survive.

Survival is our legacy.

And since we survived the Middle Passage as involuntary passengers on a trip that sealed our fate/And we survived slavery, whips and latches by learning how to give way and stay small/And we survived the Civil War by claiming freedom at the hands of those who looked like our oppressors/And we survived Jim Crow by teaching our children the unwritten rules that were marked by our blood/And we survived black mayors who moved from our communities, took a piece of our spirit but left their humanity behind—we will survive this.

And though there are times when we are like strangers in a foreign land/we look around and wonder how we got here/we take stock and realize how little we actually have/we wonder how long we will continue to suffer and die at the hands of both the oppressor and of the oppressed—we survive anyway.

There are days when I look at my sons and my heart swells with pride, As I think about all that they use to be and all that they can become, And then I stop and catch my breath/I grab my chest and clutch my pearls/I blink back tears and shake my head/because I am the mother of two black boys being raised in a post-racial world/where my cries for justice for Freddie Grey and for Tyrone West and for Sandra Bland and for Tamir Rice still get swallowed up and suppressed.

There are nights when I stand in the doorway of their room—not to wake them up for the revolution but to simply remind myself that, just for a moment, they are still safe and still here.

All I want is what every other mother wants around this city—the simple comfort of knowing that my sons' lives matter—to those who look like them and those who don't/and that my work, to pour love, light, and truth into them, will not be in vain.

And with this very simple truth/as my songs of peace get lost in my never-ending cries for justice, I know we will survive. We will rebuild. We will move on. Survival is our legacy and surviving everyday—in this system—is our goal.

# love letters from a place called baltimore

Boys:

If I could, I would write you a love letter about survival/about a time when black men, like black panthers, roamed free/about a place where black bodies are not endangered and black life is not criminalized.

The letter would weave together stories of who we used to be/ and how we are the descendants of men and women who chose to survive.

I would teach you what it means to be a survivor/even before I teach you how to write your name.

I would tell you all about how I used to be afraid of white sheets and how I wouldn't even use them on my bed. I would talk about how I started using them once folks traded them in for blue uniforms and then traded their wooden crosses for bully clubs.

I would remind you that we are a long-willed stubborn people.
We survived slavery and whips and lashes
on the backs of people like Harriet Tubman and Nat Turner
people who chose to go forward to throw their back against the
wind, to keep moving, in search of something better.

We survived sharecropping and the period called the nadir,
The Great Depression, Vietnam, Reagonomics, and crack cocaine.

We will survive Donald Trump and people like him who dream
of a divided world
of walls and signs that mark spaces for an all white America.
We will survive it all because we are survivors.

We are stubborn and strong-willed.
We survived lynchings, cross burnings, and being terrorized for
wanting to vote and for trying to reclaim our voices.
We survived Jim Crow and broke the back of small minded people

We have been beaten and starved,
Disenfranchised and disempowered,
Overlooked and ignored,
Underpaid and underrepresented.

But we have survived because we are strong-willed and stubborn.
Because that is our legacy.

We stand tall at the feet of this racist system
determined not to collapse under the pressure from the hand
that is being held against our back.
And so we stand at this place,
where guilty verdicts are meted out
  —one chokehold at a time
  —one gunshot at a time
  —one lynching at a time
  —one whipping at a time.

And still, I would remind you that we are survivors.
We are stubborn.
We                          are                          strong-willed.
We will survive because it is our legacy and it is our goal.

# black mommy activism p2

I wake up frustrated and angry everyday.
I make breakfast while yelling at the world.
You will not defeat me.
You will not break me.
You will not, not today.
I shake my fist frustrated because really who is listening.

But now,
I must confess, that every single night,
I drill my sons about their day
and then I sit for a while
and I think long and hard about our decision
to send them to school rather than to keep them with us.

I wonder how much of themselves did they lose
and how much did they gain.
I wonder if they were silenced or ignored or cut down.
I wonder if they were afraid to be creative,
scared to be too excited about learning,
I wonder if they were once again bullied,
once again the butt of all the jokes.
Did they try and disappear
or to make themselves small?

I wonder about what my older son is dealing with
as a black boy in a predominantly white environment.
And what my younger son is dealing with
as a black boy in a predominantly black environment.

I think about day prisons masquerading as schools
teachers working as prison guards
principals who believe that they are wardens.

I think of metal detectors
and black bodies being arrested or slammed to the ground.
I think about black girls sitting at their desks
and then being flipped upside down by white men
in the presence of a black man and black boys
who bore witness but bit their tongues,
choosing to remain silent.
I think about how there  are no roadblocks
erected to deny access to our bodies.

I think about the ongoing miseducation
of our Negro children and I sigh.

I wake up angry and frustrated every single day.
I pack lunches while yelling at the world.
You will not, not today.
You will not break me or defeat me today.
I shake my fist frustrated because really who is listening.

# the ghetto really ain't beautiful, really
*(with apologies to imani)*

I grew up learning how to dream
of big houses and fancy cars and simple lovers
watching too much television
on nights I should have been
enjoying the sunset.

I got too many beatings
in dark, dusty basements
not to understand that real life
sometimes hurts more than
fantasy.

I grew up watching my mother
carve our futures out of
day old bread and forgotten memories.

Ghettos are not beautiful,
even though donald trump, bill clinton, republicans, and bad poets
would have you have you think otherwise;
and those of us who grew up running
through treeless parks and concrete jungles
who had to learn how to plant daydreams in places
where liquor bottles and winos
used to lay,
know that lies cannot masquerade as truth for long.

But, I do remember being happy
even when I was sitting between

my mother's legs
with my eyes closed
holding my ears
while she attacked my kitchen
armed only with a hot comb
good intentions and processed grease.

Life was sometimes too simple
growing up with big dreams
and with high hopes
even though the world
was falling down around me;
where each step took me closer to God
and farther away from reality.

But I was still happy
and that's why I loved my mother
because she stood strong shielding me
from life's bumps and bruises,
and she sent me off to college with
$50 dollars, 2 sets of clothes,
an empty alabaster box filled with all the tears
that she shed to get me right were I was,
and the sound of her blues ringing in my ears.

She caught my tears and
turned them into sunshine
and she loved me, even at 15,
after being abused and ignored,
I couldn't even love myself.

But ghettos, I am told,
(by those much smarter than me),
are not beautiful

in places where broken glass
lays instead of cobblestones
and black love tries to make everything ok.

And despite our afros and our perms
our dashikis and our bell bottom pants
growing up in the 70s while
trying to make sense of the 60s and
getting ready for the 80s—was not easy.

The ghetto was probably not a beautiful place
although I called it home.
Pretending is what we did best.
Pretending that father knew best
even though he wasn't always around.
Pretending that gang wars were family feuds
and that your father's blows only meant
he loved you more.

Tragedy, like black thunder, use to tuck
my brother in at night,
where his pillow was his shield
and his pistol was his sword.

Life is never beautiful
when you have to eat trash to survive,
where your neighbors' leftovers
are banquet dinners,
where cardboard boxes are commodities,
and dreams are never spoken out loud.

When they finally tell my story
either after I am gone
or I am far too old to put up

too much resistance,
they'll probably talk about
how I use to line my shoes with cardboard
because the holes had gotten to big to be ignored
or how I use to bump and grind in basement parties
in high shorts and cropped shirts,
really hoping that someone down there
would see me and love me.

They will probably laugh
when they talk about my daddy
beating me outside because I sassed him
one time too many
or about how I use to ride past those
big white suburban houses
in my daddy's '65 buick
terrorizing those fat housewives
dressed in their paisley dresses and pink rollers.

They will probably never talk about
my daddy's big bear hugs
with his bruised and cut up hands from
working all night or my mother's cries
every time she sent me out into the world
and watched as small pieces of who I was supposed to be
got chipped off of me, one at a time.

They will probably tell my story
but they will never know that all the while
in the midst of growing up and being poor
and being poor while growing up
that I was quite happy
all the time or most of it anyway,
just trying, as hard as I could, to be me.

## chant to the ancestors

be still my ancestors
and rest
for in me
your spirit
shall be revived

my ancestors rest
and be still
your spirit in me
shall be revived

revived in me
your spirit shall be
so rest
my ancestors

in me
shall your spirit
be revived
so dear sweet ancestors
rest

revive,
my ancestors,
your spirit
in me
and rest

rest my ancestors

and know
that in me
your spirit
shall be revived

be still
my restless ancestors
for in me
through me
in spite of me
your spirit
will be revived

# the birth of your activism
### *04.20.15 – 04.28.15*

Day #1: We were unprepared. We saw the video, we knew who he was, and we knew that he had died. So, we went over to Freddie Grey's neighborhood, got out of the car, and when they started to march, we joined them. We did not know where we were going. We just knew that it had to be a place that was better than here and anyway, I figured, freedom is something that you have to go and get. I told you that Coretta Scott King said that each generation has to fight for and win their freedom and that we had to be prepared to fight until the end. (You wanted to google the exact phrase but we had no time.) An older black gentleman in a "BlackLivesMatter" t-shirt and long flowing dreads said that Malcolm X said that if you were not willing to die for freedom, you should take it out of your vocabulary. He then asked, "Are you two willing to die for your freedom?" You looked at me but I could not speak. Day #1, we were not ready.

Day #2: We did not know if we should go back to Freddie Grey's neighborhood. You told me that you spent the day trying to get your classmates interested but nobody wanted to talk about him, at least not yet. So we talked about it and decided to go anyway, even if it was just to bear witness. We found a few more people, standing in solidarity, talking about freedom, and wondering what else we needed to do to demand that the city sees us and hears us. We decided that tomorrow we needed to bring our own signs and we needed to pack snacks.

Day #3: We packed our bags this morning because yesterday it took us a long time to march down to City Hall and then to walk back to our car. You complained that you were tired and that justice was taking a long time to get here. We talked about Unitarian minister and abolitionist Theodore Parker who in 1853 said that the arc of the moral universe is long but it bends toward justice. "Yes," you said, "but justice is taking a long time to get here." We tried to but could not quite agree on what type of justice we were waiting for: Justice for Freddie Grey or for Eric Garner or for Tamir Rice or Tanisha Anderson or for those who have been wrongfully convicted or for those who have been failed by the public school system. As we marched, you wondered again, if justice would ever come.

Day #4: Tired and exhausted, we decided to go straight to City Hall instead of Freddie Grey's neighborhood. You had homework and wanted to sit in the car and finish it while we waited for everyone else to come down. You said your friends laughed at you in school when you tried to talk about Freddie Grey. They said it was not a big deal and wanted to know if I was making you go. You said that it is sometimes really hard being the only black boy in your class. "They don't care about Freddie Grey," you said, and then you wondered if they cared about you.

Day #5: It's Friday and you wanted to do something else. You wanted to go somewhere else and then you said you just wanted to be someone else. You said you did not want to have to care about Freddie Grey or fight for justice. "Why can't I be like the kids in my school? They are not thinking about justice for Freddie Grey or marching or praying to stay alive." I realized then that this is what racism has done to our kids, it has robbed them of their childhood. Black boys and girls are not allowed to be children, to not have a care in the world, to only think of themselves. They are born into a society where they have to fight to stay alive, fight to stay present, fight to get a good education, fight for the right to grow up, and when they become parents, the fight starts all over again.

Day #6 8a: We woke up early this morning. We wanted to be in Freddie Grey's neighborhood as early as possible. Today was going to be long and we were expecting to see thousands of people. I signed up to document what happened, video taping, taking pictures, and posting them in real time. You and your brother started writing your information on a white t-shirt because someone had told you earlier in the week that if they needed to identify your body, you should have your name and address written on your t-shirt. I wrote the number to the legal aid office on your arms just in case we got separated and you got arrested. We packed snacks and then we started to talk about the what if scenarios. We knew what happened in Ferguson, we knew that Baltimore was on the edge, and we knew that today, it was going to be crowded, tense, and emotional. We packed milk in case they used tear gas. During the Ferguson Uprising, Palestinian students tweeted out that milk was the best thing to use when you have been exposed to tear gas. We packed bandanas and snacks, extra chargers for our phones and cash. You said, "Take a picture of me so if something happens you know what I'm wearing." You laughed and said that this week, more than ever before in your life, you had gained such a deep level of respect and admiration for the foot soldiers from the Civil Rights Movement. "Just think mommy," you said, "they did this everyday."

Day #6 11a: We stood for over an hour waiting for the March to start. We walked through the crowd, greeting other protestors like they were are family members and in some ways they were. We had been out here all week and though we did not know their names, we knew that we were on the same side. Two older brothers from the Bloods walked over and told me that if something happened, they would watch out for you and your brother. He then told you that if you were afraid and you thought something was going down, than you should come and stand behind them because they had your back. He said, "Mom, don't worry, we got them." We decided to fall in line behind them because there were so many people and it was not clear who was in charge. We were told that we were heading downtown and we were going to shut the City down on our way to City Hall. A young sister standing next to me, grabbed my hand, and told me to be brave and to pass it on. We must have looked confused. She smiled and said, "Yes, be brave. Pass it on." So we did and then we started to march and chant, completely convinced that justice was going to meet us on the other side.

Day #6 5p: You have asked me twice if we should leave. We were told that a beer bottle was thrown at us and the cops are up ahead, dressed in riot gear and standing in formation. It was not clear whether we were going to make it to City Hall. We were near the Harbor and I felt like we were being herded. You wondered out loud about what was going to happen next. You said that you could feel that something had changed. Your father kept calling, strongly suggesting that we leave because it was obvious that people on both sides have decided that the Harbor was where they were going to make their stand. Another beer bottle was thrown and someone yelled, "They calling us niggers." The brother from the Bloods looked at me and said, "Uhm yea, I'm not going to be too many more niggers. Not today." We were standing still and I was trying to figure out how to get us out of there. You were scared and even though we had talked about what we should do if we got separated, if they used tear gas, if things got out of hand, you did not think any of those things would actually happen. For the first time, in a very long time, you grabbed my hand and your brother's hand. "We have to stay together." I lost my sense of direction and needed a moment to figure out exactly where we were so we could move to a location where your father could pick us up. "The cops are not responding," someone yelled, "they just standing there." Someone laughed and said, maybe they're planning to drop a bomb on us. You said, "like Move?" "Move," someone said, "Move and go where?" I caught your eye and shook my head and said no, not like Move. I kept telling myself that surely they wouldn't drop a bomb here, not down here. We started walking and someone yelled, "They up there jumping on cars." And then, "They are not going to stop us." And then, "Justice for Freddie Grey." And then, "Niggers, go home." And then, we heard the sounds of glass breaking and sirens and people yelling and people running. I thought I heard a baby crying. We ran and we got out. We made it home and when we did, you said justice is never going to get here, is it?

Day #7: Freddie Grey's Wake. There was a sign that said no pictures and no videos. I walked in by myself, you and your brother did not want to go. It was very quiet in the funeral home, people were sitting and crying and praying. I think that was his mother and I smiled at her but I didn't go over. I stepped up and looked down at him. "You could have been my son," I said very quietly, "in death your life has now found meaning." And then I left. I did not sign the book or shake anyone's hand. This should be a time for his family and his friends. I am a stranger and I do not belong here. I did not know Freddie Grey, wouldn't recognize him on the street. I am only here because I want the days of Trayvon Martin, Eric Garner, Freddie Grey—those type of days—to end.

Day #8: Freddie Grey's funeral. Too many celebrities, too many talking heads, too many people talking to us and not with us. I left because it sounded like they were telling us to calm down and wait for them to work out justice for us. I left and did not look back because mega funerals do not work for me and mouthpieces that talk about justice but are not willing to fight for it make me tired.

Day #9: You climbed into the car talking about a purge. You heard that the students at Douglass High School were planning to walk out and that they wanted all students to join them. They were planning, according to you, to take over the city and like in the movie, they were going to exercise their right to purge. "Mommy," you said, "we should go. We should make our stand." Traffic was blocked off and backed up so we decided to go home instead. I thought that we could come back out once traffic settled down, we realized much later that we could not. The city had finally reached a tipping point and from what we could gather the cops were no longer standing in formation. We sat up all night, reading social media, and listening to the news. You wanted to be out there. You said that you had been marching all week and now that real change was coming, you were at home. You thought that we should just drive around until we saw something and then get out and join them. Join them doing what, I wanted to know. "Everything," you said, "maybe we need to burn this city down for Freddie Grey." So I turned off the technology so that we could talk about justice, about Freddie Grey, about the 1968 Riots, about what happens when the tipping point has been reached, and about what is going to happen in this city once the smoke clears.

Day #10: Overnight, the city changed. I told you not to worry because Dr. King once said that the universe is on the side of justice. As we rode through Freddie Grey's neighborhood, past the CVS, cops in riot gear, preachers on bull horns, the Bloods and the Crips holding signs for #BlackLivesMatter, you quietly wondered if we are all on the same side of the universe.

## refrigerator notes
### *04.20.15 – 04.28.15*

We packed and prepared.
We made lists and tried to find ourselves along the way.
I kept telling you the same things until I had to write them down.
I put it up on the refrigerator and would point to it before we left
the house to avoid any confusion once we reached the March.
I called it my Black Mommy Activist Protest March Check List:

1. Pack a sandwich for the March because we are not stopping for snacks.
2. No, that money is not for Starbucks, it is cab money in case we get separated.
3. If they use tear gas, close your eyes, bow your head, and use the milk I packed in your bag. No, don't drink it, pour it in your eyes.
4. If we get separated, do not panic just ask one of the Bloods or Crips for help. Yes, they will help you. Trust me, they will help you.
5. If I get arrested, do not come with me, call your father for help. I will be fine. Yes, I am sure I will be fine.
6. No, you cannot stage a die-in in our living room to protest your bedtime.
7. No, you cannot go march with the Black Israelites just because you like their purple shirts.
8. No, you cannot go and take a *selfie* with the National Guard
9. Yes, when they start praying, you should keep your eyes open and do not under any circumstances, grab the hand of the person standing next to you.

10. No, I do not think it is a good idea for you to get yourself arrested as a show of solidarity for the cause.
11. No, I do not think it's counterrevolutionary if I stop for coffee on the way to the March. I am tired and it is going to be a long night.
12. Stop telling the barista that you want integrated hot chocolate. I do not think that she knows what you mean.
13. No, an iPhone 6 will absolutely not make you a better protestor.
14. Don't you dare stage a walk out during your history class just because your teacher is not talking about Freddie Grey.
15. Stop asking me how long we are going to march because we are going to do it until freedom comes.
16. Yelling "I am the next Dr. King" while doing The Whip so doesn't go together.
17. Get out of mirror practicing how you are going to look for your mug shot. I said that that was not funny the first time you did it.
18. Yes, I know that your Baseball Life Matters but you are missing practice for this march.
19. The March is not the place to try and meet girls. I know it sounds revolutionary but you are 14 and I ain't having it.
20. You can say "you have nothing to lose but your chains" all day long but you are not catching a cab and meeting me at the end of the March.

# the sound of my blues
*(for the wimyn at the dc correctional treatment facility)*

they told me not to ever tell this story
not to repeat it//not to think about it
not to ever even act like i remember
what was happening to me on those days
when king got shot
kennedy got assassinated
and x got bumped off

nobody wants to talk about
how my spirit got destroyed every time
my gun touting, marijuana smoking,
fatigue wearing revolutionary daddy
use to beat my mother
with the same intensity that sinful black folks
pray on Sunday mornings and five times
a day in rooms facing east

I wasn't supposed to hear
but I listened
to the sounds of my daddy
beating my mother's head
up against the wall

she didn't have to take it but she did
said she never knew love
could hurt so much

they told me to pretend I hadn't heard

but I listened
every time he came from the movement
pissed off at the man
looking for a much easier target

my grandmother use to dry her tears
and pat her hands
all the while teaching her how to
stand tall and swallow hard
because when he hits you
it only means he loves you more
and anyway black men faced far too
much resistance from the world to be
completely responsible for their actions

my momma use to laugh between her tears
every time she remembered the good ole' days
of cheap wine, hamburger dinners and
making out in the back seat of my
granddaddy's pickup

I wasn't supposed to ask questions
but I did
and I wanted to know
what did that have to do with the fact
that he use to beat her
every time she wanted to run
or she talked about freedom
he beat her

sometimes with the talking end of the phone
but most times he did it with his hands
so what does it mean, I wanted to know
because to me, a black man beating a black woman

conjured up images of half-picked cotton fields,
secret slave freedom rituals and babies being
pulled from black breasts by white hands

any man beating any woman made me think
about Cassandra's daddy
who used to beat her in the basement with his
frat paddle and her pants down
till she cried out to God for salvation
and that always stopped him
because her daddy was a preacher from
8 to 1 on Sundays
and 6 to 7 on Wednesday evenings

but what does this have to do with
my daddy beating my momma
on his way to beating me
every time I talked back, rolled my eyes,
or put my hands on my hips

what does it have to do with his slaps meeting
her screams on lonely Saturday nights
and blues filled Monday mornings
"nothing," my mother would say
whenever we talked about it, "nothing at all"

she never seemed to understand
that silence always equals death
in a world where you die if you are silent
and for every one silent sister
many more are beaten into submission every single day

"nothing" she keeps on telling me
hoping to convince herself as she works

on convincing me, "nothing at all."

he was just overworked and underpaid
the movement demanded much more
than he was prepared to give,

"nothing at all,"
he was just a little tired
because he really wanted to give us the best
even though he never could tell what the best
of anything ever looked like

"but," I would say
as I buried my head into the pillow
drowning out the screams because
I could not stop them,
"what does this have to do with
me being pregnant with your pain and mine,
drunk with your tears and mine,
overcome with your sorrows and mine?"

"nothing," she would say,
patting my hands
eyes fixed somewhere beyond me,
"nothing at all."

# meditations
*(for the McNair Scholars)*

You must commit yourself to being hope
for those who have none,
a lighthouse in the midst of a storm,
and a compass that points the way.

You must be a road that diverges from the well-worn path,
a safe house for those who need a resting place,
and an inn that is never full.

You who have been trained and prepared; loved and nurtured.

You must become a scholar in pursuit of new questions,
a pilgrim in search of the *magis*,
and a voice that speaks the truth (no matter the cost).

You who have been well trained, prepared, loved, and nurtured.

You must become a light that finds its way into every corner,
a gear that shifts and moves us forward,
and the spark the we need to set the world on fire.

You who have been trained/prepared/loved/nurtured—
you must live a life that is, in the end, well lived.

McNair Scholars, you must commit yourself to be-ing.
Commit yourself to be.
Commit yourself.
Commit.

And then, in the end,
(right before the lights have dimmed
and the curtains have closed;
before your story has ended and your period has been placed)
you must commit to sharing what you have learned
to training the next generation of warrior scholars
and after that is done,
to gently give up the mantle of leadership
before you go quietly into the night.

**my groove echo: 11.23.15**
*(for jordan davis, forever 17)*

We are not invisible
simply because you refuse to see us.
We will not stop fighting
simply because you demand our obedience.
We will not stop dancing
simply because you refuse to hear our song.

We will not give up
simply because you want us to believe
that power/concedes without a struggle.

We are not going to forfeit our voices
simply because you are tired of hearing our words.
We will not stop shouting
simply because you try to cut out our tongues.
We will not stop coming
simply because you hold up your palm.

We will not continue to be what you are trying to create,
it is an experiment gone wrong
you will not be able to will or wish us away
simply because you refuse to recognize our humanity.
We are little miracles having conquered the art of survival.
We have learned to swallow our pain
and then use it to spark our genius.

## my ounce of truth benefits

*(with kevin amissah)*

It is tiring being me, as
I have been black all day.

My ounce of truth does benefit
And ripple and Gives voice to my pain.
My history has been written,
my life is not my own.

I am not a shadow, a figment, an apparition.
I am not invisible, simply because you choose not to see me.

Mylifematters itmatters itmatters itdoes

When I react, I am an animal.
When I am silent, I am violated.
When I fight back, I am a thug.

My ounce of truth benefits
and ripples and Gives voice to my pain.

When I am quiet, I am feared.
When I am successful, I am the exception.
When I fail, I am the rule.
When I try, I am mocked.

It is tiring being me, as
I have been black all day.

I have learned how to stand up straight,
while holding the stereotypes of the world on my shoulders.

My ounce of truth does benefit
And ripple and Gives voice to my pain.

When I arrive, I am told I do not belong.
When I do not go, I am told that I make bad choices.
When I move or shrug or walk or speak or dance,
I am your worst fear being bought to life.

I am the boogey man for the entire world.
Responsible for everything,
Yet incapable and unable to change anything.

My ounce of truth benefits
And though it doesn't fit your story
It defines my life.
It ripples and Gives voice to my pain.

It is tiring being me, as
I have been black all day.

# and this I once believed

## 2008

In 1954, on the day after the United States Supreme Court ruling, black people all over the country woke up believing that the world was no longer black and white but it was finally brown. They were excited but they were wrong. They slowly began to realize that the decision of nine white men did not change the minds of a Jim Crow nation. Today, with the election of Barack Obama, the world – for the first time – is no longer black and white. Today, with the support of all people and the votes of millions of people, the world is finally brown. And I am truly grateful. My son asked me to vote for Obama and when I asked him why – he replied, "Because he is brown and he looks like me." I thought about that for a while and realized that with the election of Obama, the color of my son's world will never be the color of mine or the color of my father's. My grandmother, who voted by absentee ballot in the state of South Carolina, sat up until midnight determined not to go to bed until she was sure that the world was finally brown. My father, who remembers growing up in the South under the yoke of Jim Crow, woke up crying at 4:30a, ready to cast his ballot to change the color of the world. The world is finally brown, which does not mean that racism has ended or sexism is over or that everything in the world is ok – it just means that America, as a whole, has finally decided that they will judge our leaders by the content of their character and not the color of their skin. The world is finally brown and I am truly grateful.

## 2015

And now more than ever before the world is blacker and whiter than it has ever been. How do you speak into the spaces that demand our attention? The spaces where black boys and girls are being killed, black voices are being suppressed, and black people are shouting and trying to prove to the world that their lives matter. Everyday we work hard to lean into those spaces where people are profiting from our pain, documenting and marking our deaths while simultaneously disregarding or ignoring our lives; those spaces where people that don't look like us feel comfortable speaking for us and over us and then call themselves our allies; those spaces where we moan and cry, and moan and cry because the hardest part of our day is the simple act of leaving the house. I was wrong in 2008 and when I should have been preparing my boys how to fight and how to be RaceBrave, I was protecting them and pandering them and pampering them. They were not ready when Trayvon was murdered and truthfully, neither was I. I should have been singing Black Lives Matter instead of We Shall Overcome. I should have been creating black powerful spaces instead of integrating white ones. I should have homeschooled my boys rather than send them to private schools. I should have given them the tools they need to carve out their lives instead of doing it for them. I should have been a racebrave mom instead of a baseball mom. I now know that the world is deeply divided. It is neither black nor white nor brown; but, it is a motley shade of gray. And, I have to learn how to live in it and then how to change it.

# speaking my truth, finally
*(stories from the archives)*
*(What Michelle once told me...)*

She said: I have held onto this story for 25 years, pretending as if it was not waiting to be told. It wakes me up at night finding its way into my dreams. It distracts me when I think about my life and try to work out a difficult problem and all I am really thinking about is that.

It is my white elephant, the truncheon that sits on my chest, the reason why I found it so hard to commit. I felt like I had no choice and I do not say that because I want to remain blameless but because I felt that there were no other options for me, at all.

I was in my first semester of college, having been sent there with the weight of my father's dreams sitting heavily on my back. I had spent the summer saying good-bye to my boyfriend and preparing myself for the next adventure of my life.

I was in college and my life, as I imagined it would always be, was starting again. But I knew that something had happened, that a gear had shifted and my life would never be the same again. It was not a test that confirmed it. I never had morning sickness or experienced dizziness. I just knew it with a quiet certitude. I was pregnant. I was someone's mother and I did not want to be. So I pretended that it was not real while thinking of ways that I could try and free myself.

I thought of throwing myself down the stairs but I was afraid that in fighting the baby I would be ruining myself. I took to sleeping on my stomach, hard. I would push into my mattress and demand that whatever was inside of me find a way to get free. I was the Underground Railroad hiding secrets in plain sight. I wore big clothes and studied and tried to pretend that I was just like everyone else.

I never mentioned it though I thought about it every moment of every day. It was five months before I looked myself in the mirror and said the words that I thought would end my life—I am pregnant and I am stuck. I told my boyfriend that weekend, crying and feeling very ashamed. We have to get an abortion, he said. I couldn't speak because he said we but he meant you. He would not have to do it. He had not been dealing with feeling like his body had turned against him. He said we and though the conversation moved on and we begin to plan, I stayed right there at that moment.

I told my mother and because she is used to disappointment and heartache she did not blink, did not cry, did not even do what I really wanted her to do but I could not say. I wanted her to put her arms around me and tell me that I was not going through this alone and to tell me that I was going to be ok. I wanted her to be my anchor, my rock, my simple place of solitude in this storm that had become my life.

She asked instead about money, did he have any. I called him and he came over with $100 dollars, ten wrinkled and damp ten-dollar bills. They felt sticky like he had been sitting there holding it while waiting for me to call. It felt like he had been crying over the bills, hoping that this would be a physical end to his nightmare. He seemed relieved when he gave it to me, like his part, his responsibility had been satisfied. I never heard from him again.

My mom began to make plans, sounding cold almost uncaring She asked me how many months. I said, I think five. She looked at me sharply and then she just looked away. Again, I felt ashamed. She said, as she shook her head almost in disbelief at this child this woman who had been lying to herself and to the world, that at five months we had to go to the emergency room. They did a sonogram and I turned my head so that I would not have to see. I would not have to believe. I could continue to just be a spectator. I was not a participant, I kept telling myself.

The doctor spoke only to my mom and told her that we would have to go to New York because that was the closest city that would do it. He said, she is 20 weeks and if you had come two weeks ago. And she is so close to the end, maybe she wants to keep it. My mother answered for me, cutting off that train, where in New York. There is a hospital, he said, for women who are this far along, just one though, and you need to go this week. If you wait any longer then even they will not do it. She is 20 weeks and soon it will not be safe.

It was not safe though I did survive. I had to go through labor, had to pass the baby through, had to lay there, separated only by a curtain and listen to everyone else's cries and moans. The told me to take a walk and that was when it happened. I remember collapsing and apologizing and feeling once again, ashamed.

It was not safe though I did survive. I saw it as a war and that neither one of us were going to win but only one of us would be standing at the end. I remember that I was prepared to kill us both, if that meant I would be free. My mother never mentioned what happened to me. She simply took me back to campus, put me in the bed, kissed my forehead, and left.

I remember that I could not stop crying. I could not eat. I

could not sleep. I just laid in my bed, moaning and holding my stomach, regretting the life I had chosen to call my own. I had been someone's mother and selfishly, I chose not to be. I prayed for forgiveness and it took months, it took years, it took decades before I could forgive myself and write about my pain.

I write her letters all the time, the scared frightened lonely teenager that I used to be and I tell her to be strong. I tell her to be racebrave, to forgive herself. I tell her that I love her and that I am at peace with her decision and then, I thank her for choosing to survive. Her choices, her decisions have helped me to mother the boys that I chose to keep, with clarity with a fierceness and with a desire to give up everything I have so that they can grow up and be free.

# your silence will not protect you
*diary 01.19.15*

Today I am sad to say that I am not doing enough to fight for freedom, to fight for justice, to fight for the true application of #BlackLivesMatter.

And to fight against oppression; to fight against racism; to fight against sexism; to fight against classism; to fight against my feelings of despair, of helplessness, of hopelessness, of anger, of frustration; to fight for my boys, for their future, and for their right to live free happy whole safe lives.

Today, as I read through lesser-known more radical more socialist more Black Lives Matter-toned speeches written by Dr. King, I realize that I am really not doing enough and if I want to help make the world a better place, I must change.

*I write so that I can breathe, so that I can feel like I am doing something, so that I can exhale, so that I can remind myself that I am still here.*

## your silence will not protect you
*diary 02.15.16*

Last night, every time I fell asleep, I woke up crying and sweating, and absolutely terrified that something had happened to my sons. I spent the entire night running back and forth between their room and mine. Even when I stood at the door of their room, I didn't calm down until I shook them, just a bit, to make sure that they were still breathing. The pattern kept repeating itself until I finally made a palette on the floor of their room and sat there reading and watching them all night. My heart breaks for the mother of TamirRice, TyroneWest, MikeBrown, TrayvonMartin, JohnCrawford, EzellFord, DanteParker, TanishaAnderson, RumainBrisbon, AkaiGurley, JerameReid, TonyRobinson PhillipWhite, EricHarris, RekiaBoyd, EricGardner, DontreHamilton, AiyanaJones, JordanDavis—because my horrible nightmare is their reality. #BlackChildrenMatter

After the murder of TrayvonMartin, my sons wanted to know "Mommy, what are we going to do?" They asked that question as they begin to record, on their bedroom wall, the names of every unarmed black person who was killed by rogue cops or would be vigilantes. The list kept growing and growing and they kept asking me. We would speak the names of the victims into the wind and they kept asking me. We would pray for their families and still, they kept asking me. When FreddieGrey was murdered, they stopped asking and began to tell me what we could to do to be involved.

I mark that as the moment that their activist spirit, the one I had been nurturing and feeding and cultivating from the time that they could read and write, was finally released.

*I had to keep reminding myself that even when everything in me is calling out for me to remain quiet, I must push past it because my silence (no matter how scared I am or what I will lose by speaking up) will not protect me —either from them or from myself. And if I have raised my boys right, they will choose to claim and fight for the right to claim ownership over their voices.*

# your silence will not ~~protect you~~

*diary 08.15.15*

I am wrestling with my mourning.
2015 has been just that kind of year.
Everyday I woke up to news that left me
tired, frustrated, ready to fight, and angry
—very very angry.

This country, this city,
became a racial battleground
my people are being stalked and killed
hunted and herded
and then racist bystanders
publicly malign them
because they have the audacity
to demand justice
because justice is finally due.

*I truly believe that I am suffering from PTPRD (post-traumatic post racial disorder). I can barely sleep at night and am sometimes terrified to let my teenage black boys out of my sight. Racism is a wool and itchy blanket and I am being smothered by it. Smothered to death.*

# your silence ~~will not protect you~~

*diary 06.10.15*

My Testimony: Lately every morning I wake up angry and frustrated, emotionally spent and overwhelmed. I feel like I am in middle of an ongoing war to completely remove black people from this space.

The photo of Dejerrica Becton in a bikini being physically, emotionally, and spiritually held down with a grown white man's knee on her back was my undoing.

That image made me think about rape, abuse, slavery, and the uncontested access that all men seem to have to a black woman's or black girl's body.

When she cried for her mother, I remembered all the times when I was a young girl and grown men assaulted me with their sexual innuendos, their inappropriate hugs, and their eyes—that lingered far too long on my itty bitty chest and I cried for and to my mother.

I remembered being told that it was my fault when grown men grabbed their crotches and yelled out to me as I walked down the street.

I remember feeling ashamed as I transitioned from girl to woman and I was told that I could not climb trees, participate in spitting contests, or get loud because that is not what proper young girls do.

I remember trying to name my abusers and being told that some things are best left unsaid. I remember having to write down every abusive incident so that I would not forget.

I am an older weather worn Dejerrica Becton and I will Say Her Name and I will speak up for her because all I wanted when I was a young black girl growing up in America was for someone to speak up for me.

*We need to practice daily acts of resistance—even if it is only resistance to the sickness that is America. To the racism that is America. To the sexism that is America. We practice resistance until we get it right.*

## your ~~silence will not protect you~~
*(for tamir rice)*
*diary 12.12.15*

Justice is not blind.

It sees that we are black and then, as always, it rules against us.
Grown folks are now debating and discussing and justifying why
it was ok for him to be shot and killed while he was in a park,
playing all by himself.

This is what racism looks like.

This is why I fight and march and scream and pray.
This is why I yell #BlackLivesMatter, at the top of my lungs,
working hard to drown out the #AllLivesMatter choir. This is why
I pray my head off every time my teenage boys leave the house.

He was not invisible simply because you refused to see him.

And neither are we/neither are we. We will not stop speaking
simply because you demand our submission. We will not give
up simply because you want us to believe that change happens
without hard work. We are not going to forfeit our voices/simply
because you are tired of hearing our cries.

We cannot breathe or grow in a box.

We will not continue to be the cancer of this world, in need of
radioactive waves of racism to keep us at bay, the reasons why you
cry and pray, simply because you just refuse to see us.

We will continue to sing about the beauty of the world we want to create with our own song.

# your silence will not protect you
*diary 01.10.16*

*"Nearly 90% of the homicides in Baltimore City (in 2015) were the result of shootings...more than 90% of victims were black... more than 90% were boys and men...more than half were between the ages of 18-30." – City Paper*

2015, Baltimore City: We fought multiple battles to keep our children alive; to keep them healthy; to provide them with decent housing, healthy food options, mental health services, safe and clean environments, and decent (though I would prefer stellar) educational opportunities. A battle that we did not win.

2016, Baltimore City: We must try harder; we must do better. Black Lives Matter Baltimore must continue to be a rallying cry, a shield, a blanket, a way of life, a challenge to the old regime, an ushering in of new and fresh ideas—it must be the point where we make our stand and commit to being the ones that we have been waiting for; the ones who are willing to fight against those who are outside of our community and then show up and shoot and kill us with impunity and those within our community who are more committed to being a part of the problem rather than the solution.

What am I doing to be a change agent? What am I doing be a part of the solution? What am I willing to do to make things better? What am I willing to give up? And when do I plan to start? I keep asking myself the same questions every night all night.

*This is our city, these are our streets, these are our children, and this is our battle. We must all win or we will all lose.*

# comfedderate flag memories

**June 1980**

Dear diary:

Today Peter told me that we couldnt play together anymore. Youre a yankee nigger, and you need to back north. He said that they were proud comfedderates and I needed to be scared because the south was going to rise again. I told him I wasn't afraid and that I aint no chicken. I am scared diary because whats a comfedderate? Should I tell my daddy? Will the comfedderates get him too?

**June 2015**

Every time I see that flag something dies inside of me. It is a symbol of hate of oppression of a time when we were cattle. It reminds me that people were willing to fight to the death rather than recognize that we were human. I remember growing up and seeing the flag painted on the sides of pick up trucks driven by white boys who would call me a nigger as they rode by. It was hanging outside of homes where my neighbors would host parties and invite everyone on the block but us. It was mounted in stores where we bought our bread, hung up on the walls next to framed whites only and colored only signs. It is easy to blame the flag for racist white men who shoot black people in churches but I would rather blame the core of hatred and fear that sits at the center of the heart of racism. Someone lied to him along the way, someone told him he was special, someone led him to believe that the world that they had once heard about (the one where whiteness rules) was possible.

**September 2015**

And now this, I pull into carpool comfortable in my self-induced Duke Ellington and Ella Fitzgerald afternoon haze. You cut in front of me, waving me off with your hand, and leaving a stench that makes it way into my rolled up windows from the Confederate flag stickers that are plastered across your trunk. I write this poem and leave it in my car because the next time, I will be ready.

I see you/I hear you/I know you
You were not born this backwards
For this, I look to all who led you to
believe that the earth revolved around
you instead of around the sun.
The South, my friend, will not rise again,
dinosaurs will not walk this earth again,
and you will see me again
And I will be ready.
We will talk and I will drag you,
kicking and screaming,
into the light of a new day
(the one where the #BlackLivesMatter bulb shines bright
and confederate flags are a thing of the past!).

# morning drive time

My youngest son (speaking softly): "Hear the shots, cut off the light, stack the books, hit the floor, go up against the wall, close my eyes, pray..."

*I glance over at him for just for a moment and*

"Open one eye, look for her, if she's next to you, grab her hand, tell her it's going to be ok..."

*I open my mouth to speak but*

"Don't try to be a hero, get out of here alive, you're a Whitehead, you're a survivor."

*then I close it.*

"God bless you Amir, they will know your name. You will not be a hash tag. Mommy won't make a t-shirt with your face on it."

*I pull over to pray, to collect myself, to just sit in solidarity with him.*

"I am more than a hash tag. I am more than a movement. I am more than that. They can't kill us all. They can't kill us all. They can't kill us all." (leaning his head back and closing his eyes) "They can't kill us all."

> *I begin to drive because there is nothing to say.*
> *My reality once again meets me face-to-face,*
> *as I am raising two black boys in America*

*and I send them out everyday*
*without bulletproof vests or hand grenades.*
*They go out without shields or swords.*
*They are unarmed but have been baptized in my prayers,*
*in my silent hopes of a safer world.*
*I send them out even though I am afraid,*
*even though I can barely speak,*
*even though I have to bite my fist to keep from screaming out,*
*even though have to bite my tongue to keep from yelling out,*
*even though I spend every moment of every day laying down my*
*burdens,*
*and, even though I know that I alone cannot save them,*
*I send them out anyway.*

"They can't kill us all."

*And yet, and yet, and yet, I send them out anyway.*

# sunday morning service
*(for sandra bland)*

We say your name
because we know they want you to be erased
to be just a memory
to be just a fragment
to be just a fragrance caught in their wind.

We chant your name
because we could not stop your arrest.
We saw it but could not act
as throwing stones at a computer never changes anything.

We whisper your name, over and over again,
because we still strive to find the normal
to give voice to our pain
to reclaim what we love
to remember who we are.

We whisper it, over and over again,
because there is a sore—
festering raw infested real—called racism
that has always been there
covered up for years by enslavement by reconstruction
by the nadir
covered up for years by segregation by voting rights
by amendments
uncovered finally by the stench that is post-racial.

We sing your name

because we have come to the place where we must be held
accountable.
We didn't want you to just be a hash tag,
a name thrown around by politicians
who want our vote but not our voices but we let it happen,
we couldn't stop it.

We will stand on your name
because we have learned how to sit quietly and meditatively
at the feet of your memory
but we will not set up a tent and remain there
for there is no time for rest, not just yet.

the baltimore riots
baltimore's fire next time
## baltimore's Uprising—at last

we are baltimore.
bold. black. brazen.
we are complicit if we do not struggle
if we do not fight for justice
if we do not stand up against oppression
we wake up blinking and disoriented
at what happened to FreddieGrey
as if TyroneWest had never happened

we cry out for an end to injustice
we who want balance to be restored
we who are waiting for freedom to happen
we who are living on two parts of an old dream
$1/5^{ths}$ of a mayor's empty promise
soul filled remnants of a castrated spirit

we must remain awake
and not sleep through the world's greatest revolution
we are blackbaltimore
we must practice daily acts of resistance
around systems of oppression

begrudged. beguiled.
a stained replica of a teary eyed memory
verses of an unsung love song
stanzas of hope filled blues
we sing their blues

we sing our blues

rambling through the soil of this city
destitute travelers with lines drawn that cannot be crossed
searching for a time once forgotten
crown prince messiahs desperately trying to find ourselves
trading sunbeams, as it were, for a song

truth glistening from our eyes
compassion does define our spirit
we dance to a tune that only we can hear
in the midst of the center
of a war torn city
buildings are on fire
curfews are maintained
communities, as always, divided

we are who you are frightened of becoming
a manifestation of your very worst daymares
downtrodden bums carving out a righteous experience

we are who you have forced us to become
a blood stained blemish
of dreams long deferred
festering in the shadows
floating silently through our pain

come and fly with us
through the meadows of our mind
we are baltimore.
jagged edges. imperfect. flawed.
but this is our life/our home
and we must claim it as our own

# Section II

black love is black wealth

# we are gathered
*(for bishop billie kearns bamberg)*

I stand here today to celebrate and honor the life and legacy of a man who walked this journey for 62 years as a black man in America, never wavering and never giving up. I stand here today to be among the people who have been shaped and nurtured and loved and disciplined and ministered and cared for by him.

I stand here today as a member of a family who is gathered together. We are gathered because it is not unusual to come together to honor people that we love, to seek comfort from one another in our hours of need. We gather to draw upon his strength and add it to our years. We gather so we can keep going and gaining and reaping and knowing and understanding. We gather so that we can sing the songs that we remember and recite the psalms that we were taught. We are gathered.

We gather to celebrate his hands. The same hands that picked you up when you had fallen, that wiped away your tears. Those hands. The ones you grabbed when you needed to cross the street, the ones that reached back to pull us forward. The ones that prayed with you, prayed over you, and prayed for you. Those hands. The ones that can take day old bread and turn it into sunshine and Sunday dinner. Those hands, that have known plowing, digging, planting, pruning and patching. We gather to celebrate them and give thanks.

The family gathers to celebrate his childhood, growing up in the clay and dust and sand of South Carolina, picking pecans, running free, weaving stories, playing make believe. It is easy to remember when he first taught you things that you have never forgotten.

We gather to celebrate his laugh and how it sounded like it came from his soul. His laugh said, "I've seen freedom coming for a long time and it ain't here but it's closer than its every been." Hearing him laugh and be happy and be in the moment made us laugh so we gather to remember.

The family is gathered here today because we have to because gathering is what we do best. It is the essence of who we are. We gather now to celebrate his eyes and the way they looked when he smiled at you and you knew that you were loved. His eyes saw so much. He has seen his daughter and nieces and nephews grow up and get married and have kids of their own. He has seen it all. He has seen us be who we really are and even when we thought no one was looking—he was.

We are gathered here because of his 62 years, which is a lot of breathing, of taking in and giving out. It is a lot of space, of making friendships that lasted forever, of planting roots that have sprouted generations and of working and working and working until you can't work anymore. It is a lot of walking and driving, of laughing and crying, of births and funerals, of sermons and weddings. It is a long time to fly when everyone else is depending upon you to soar high and lead the way. We are gathered here to remember and to give thanks for his years of loving and laughing, of giving and receiving, of teaching and of learning, and of simply being the best of who he was time and time again.

The family gathers here to remember his voice, so strong so Southern. A voice that reminded me, even on the darkest of days, of sunshine. He had a voice that lifted you up, that spoke to your pain and supported your joy. He had a voice that commanded attention. His voice could stop you when you were on your way to doing something wrong. We are gathered here because he took those words and made them his own and told us who we were. We are gathered here for him.

The family gathers here because it is a part of our nature to want to be together in times of mourning, sharing and shouldering one another's hurt and pain. We are gathered here to remember his dreams. When we began this journey as wide-eyed innocent happy babies; as toddlers; as children we dream of changing the world, climbing every mountain and of conquering every obstacle. And year by year, as we crawled, then walked, then ran and then began to walk again but much much slower this time—we realized that although we could not change the world, we could change ourselves and sometimes all mountains are not meant to be climbed and some obstacles like racism and Jim Crown and inadequate housing and poor educational facilities might not be completely conquered by us alone. He was a man with a lot of dreams. He accomplished some, put away a few, adjusted one or two, and passed many of them onto others, his spiritual sons and daughters. We are gathered here, as a fulfillment of his dreams and as a reminder that though he is absent in the body, his dreams, which are in all of us, are not. So we gather.

The family is gathered and this is not new, for we are a people who gather together. We are here today because he was a man of God and we honor that and cling to that and hold on to that because those of us who believe, shall meet him again. He was tired and weary and his bones ached from living and pushing and going for so long. There comes a point when your spirit realizes that in this place, you have seen it all, heard it all, said it all, laughed too long and cried too much and it is now time to go home. We are gathered here not to mourn, but to celebrate. We are gathered here as a family to simply say, "Good night, we will see you in the morning."

# a regenerative descant
### (for sergeant major o'neal johnson, jr.)

standing still
retirement after three decades will result in a lot
of days of standing still
sunshine, a lot of days to exhale and wait
to see the sun rise, discover new past times,
rediscover old ones

how do we celebrate a soldier who has put
his life on the line for close to thirty years, who has
worked hard on behalf of the people, who has redefined
what it means to be an unsung hero
thereby giving the universe an insight into
what it means to sacrifice

heroes are all cut from the same tree
not logs, scraps of wood, or toothpicks
but molded and sculptured
translating their art onto the roots
of long life, baobab trees having
endured the hurricanes, volcanoes,
and earthquakes
from life in America

we are a short memoried people
much too willing to settle for artless resumes of
rapid life   brief prayers     lattes
we are unwilling to take life slow
to stand up and be counted

to have a voice and make a stand
to seek, time and time again, the impossible

our young adapt without question, so therefore,
we fail to acknowledge brilliance among us
displaying a hesitancy to tell this soldier,
this good brother
how his journey has become our journey

we must read this man differently
soldiers must and should be
held to a different standard

they know how to look and reach beyond
they know how to tow the line
how not to give way, or give in, or give up
failure is never an option
as, there are some things
more important than your life

this soldier, after 30 years
of obedience and service
possesses a deep-rooted joy, easy laughter,
he takes time to hear and to mentor
those who gratefully and gracefully
walk in his shadow

he has come of age in a military community
his unit understood and they called him sir
they think he is a mountain
we know that he is a precious stone; a descant

we are a short memoried people,
and he has been planted among us

artfully seeded in good soil to illuminate our texts,
shepherd our prayers, spiritualize our commitments, and help
us heal the holes in our souls.

# life's longing for itself
### (for mercedes, kofi, & amir)

take my voice and make it yours.
take my courage and claim it as your own.
find yourself in the stiches I call my life.

my love for you gets choked in my throat,
never knowing how to say I love you,
I cant even get that right.

mothering is hard work.
I have failed at moments
when failure really shouldnt have been an option.
But I, I got back up
and then I got back up
and then I got back up again.

And I tried,
to love you to see you to find you
to cut through my layers of pain
of childhood memories
of missed opportunities
of words spoken in earnest
that can never be taken back.

Im sorry never seemed like enough to say.
(apologies sound empty when they come wrapped in pain)
I look at you and I see the best
of who I had one day hoped to become.
if I could have polished out the unfinished edges of a life
that I have called my own.

I see your scars, the roadmaps to your pain
and I can trace them back
sometimes, to me.
I did not protect you from me/
from the world or from yourself.

your life has always been your own.
I once prayed for answers
to the questions I had about my life
and God, in his wisdom, sent me you.

## soulmates and soulfood

*(kuro ai #1: for you)*

sometimes when I wake up
long before brushing my teeth
gathering my thoughts or feeding my cat

thoughts of you flood my mind
springing from my soul
to fall gently from my lips

## soulmates and soulfood

*(kuro ai #2)*

you speak like wild flowers blooming
stretching forth to capture my soul
in the essence of you

I wake up and put on your love
and like an armor it cloaks me
lending me the strength I need
to face another day

# soulmates and soulfood

*(kuro ai #3)*

I know I love you
because every time you leave
I make plans for getting past tomorrow

I know I need you
because every time you enter a room
a piece of my spirit stands in reverence to your love

# soulmates and soulfood
*(kuro ai #4)*

I used to be
invisible until
you started seeing me

So, I know Im gonna marry you
because you are the only man
who has ever really seen me
and loved me anyway

And I know we gonna grow old together
because you are the one
I have been waiting for

## soulmates and soulfood
*(kuro ai #5)*

I woke up listening
to the sound of you sleeping

the rise and fall of your breath
lulling me gently back to sleep

and I started thinking
of how revolutionary it really was

to wake up in a cold house
under a warm blanket

to the sound of a black man at peace

# black love + you&me = black wealth

*(with a quiet nod to zora)*
*(for whitehead, 10.02.99)*

after tossing and turning all night
worried fretful concerned
about our life and our bills and our kids
I sat up quietly

not wanting to wake you
not wanting your day to begin
before it was time

you are smiling as you roll over
away from the peek of the sun
through our well-worn shade

I watch you
still in awe of you
still in love with you
seventeen years of laugh lines and grey hairs
and you are still my dream catcher
and my heart gets snagged every time I see you

but I am no romantic
never dreamed of waiting for a man
on a white horse
to swoop in and save me

and I don't eat apples
so I never had a fear of being poisoned

and needing a man on a white horse
to swoop in and wake me

but you,
you make me want to rewrite
my childhood stories
substituting cinderella for shaniqua
prince charming for leroy
lush green forests for concrete jungles
wicked witches for politicians
poisoned apples for crack cocaine
evil stepmothers who have lost their way
    for heartless mayors who have lost their way
attending late night balls in plump gowns, glass slippers
    for basement blue light parties in crop tops, daisy dukes

you make me want to believe
that black love is black wealth
and that in the end
your love for me will be both an anchor
that tethers me to your shore

and a balloon that allows me to soar
as I, try over and over again,
to jump at the sun
just so that I can pretend to fly
in the moment when my feet finally leave the ground

# Section III

today…again

# today my heart stopped

7.17.14 Eric Garner;

8.5.14 John Crawford III; 8.9.14 Michael Brown Jr.;

8.11.14 Ezell Ford; 8.13.14 Dante Parker;

11.13.14 Tanisha N. Anderson; 11.21.14 Akai Gurley;

11.23.14 Tamir E. Rice; 12.02.14  Rumain Brisbon;

12.31.14 Jerame C. Reid; 1.8.15 Artago Damon Howard;

1.23.15 Demaris Turner; 2.5.15 Jeremy Lett;

2.15.15 Lavall Hall; 2.19.15 Janisha Fonville;

3.1.15 Thomas L. Allen Jr.; 3.1.15 Charly Leundeu Keunang;

3.6.15 Tony Terrell Robinson; 3.6.15 Andrew Anthony Williams;

3.6.15 Naeschylus Vinzant; 3.9.15 Anthony Hill;

3.11.15 Terry Garnett Jr.; 3.12.15 Robert Gross;

3.19.15 Brandon Jones; 3.24.15 Nicholas Thomas;

3.30.15 Ricky Shawatza Hall (Mya) Hall; 3.31.15 Phillip White;

4.2.15 Eric Courtney Harris; 4.4.15 Walter Scott;

4.14.15 Colby Robinson; 4.15.15 Frank Ernest Shephard III;

4.19.15 Freddie Gray; 4.22.15. William L. Chapman II;

4.25.15 David Felix; 5.6.15 Brendon Glenn;

5.7.15 Nephi Arriguin; 5.9.15 Sam Matthew Holmes;

5.11.15 Lionel Lorenzo Young; 5.11.15 Kelvin Antonie Goldston;

5.12.15 D'Angelo Reyes Stallworth;  6.11.15 Fritz Severe;

6.13.15 Deng Manyoun; 6.15.15 Kris Jackson;

6.16.15 Christopher DeLeon;

*6.17.15 Depayne Middleton-Doctor\*Cynthia Hurd\**
*Susie Jackson\*Ethel Lance\*Clementa Pinckney\*Tywanza Sanders\**
*Daniel Simmons Sr.\*Sharonda Coleman-Singleton\*Myra Thompson;*

6.25.15 Spencer Lee McCain;

7.1.15 Kevin Lamont Judson; 7.13.15 Sandra Bland…

**today…again and again**\*

\*from http://killedbypolice.net

# About the Author

Karsonya Wise Whitehead, Ph.D. author of the award-winning *Notes from a Colored Girl: The Civil War Pocket Diaries of Emilie Frances Davis*, has also written *Letters to My Black Sons: Raising Boys in a Post-Racial America* and *Sparking the Genius: The 2013 Carter G. Woodson Lecture*; and is the co-editor of *Rethinking Emilie Frances Davis: Lesson Plans for Teaching Her 1863-1865 Civil War Pocket Diaries*. She is an associate professor of Communication and African and African American Studies at Loyola University Maryland; a K-12 master teacher in African American History; an award-winning curriculum writer and lesson plan developer; an award-winning former Baltimore City middle school teacher; and, a three-time New York Emmy-nominated documentary filmmaker.

From 2013-2015, Dr. Whitehead was selected as one of only four experts to participate in the White House's Black History Month Panel co-sponsored by President Obama and the Association for the Study of African American Life and History (ASALH). She has received numerous awards and honors including the University of Notre Dame's Kroc Institute for International Peace Studies 2016 "Distinguished Alumni" Award for her work as a peace activist, scholar, filmmaker, writer, and poet; the 2014 Lifetime Achievement Award from the Progressive National Baptist Convention (PNBC); and, Loyola University Maryland's 2013 Faculty Award for Excellence in Engaged Scholarship, for her work documenting the stories of women who are temporarily experiencing homelessness. She has also received both the Langston Hughes, David Diop, Etheridge Knight Poetry Award (1999 and 2000) and the Zora Neale Hurston Creative Writing Award (1998) from the Gwendolyn Brooks Creative

Writing Center at the University of Chicago. In 2007, Whitehead was selected as the Gilder Lehrman Preserve America Maryland History Teacher of the Year Award (sponsored by the Gilder Lehrman Institute of American History and the Maryland State Department of Education).

In 2015, *Notes from a Colored Girl* was awarded the Darlene Clark Hine Book Award for Best Book in African American women's and gender history from the Organization of American Historians (OAH) and, in 2014, it was awarded the Letitia Woods Brown Book Award for Best Edited Book in African American History from the Association of Black Women Historians (ABWH).

Dr. Whitehead is an in-demand motivational speaker, a prolific blogger, and a frequent guest on radio and television. She can be reached on her website https://kayewisewhitehead.com/; by e-mail griotonthego@gmail.com; on twitter @kayewhitehead; and, through her Facebook fan page. She lives in Baltimore with her family and her dog.

Apprentice House is the country's only campus-based, student-staffed book publishing company. Directed by professors and industry professionals, it is a nonprofit activity of the Communication Department at Loyola University Maryland.

Using state-of-the-art technology and an experiential learning model of education, Apprentice House publishes books in untraditional ways. This dual responsibility as publishers and educators creates an unprecedented collaborative environment among faculty and students, while teaching tomorrow's editors, designers, and marketers.

Outside of class, progress on book projects is carried forth by the AH Book Publishing Club, a co-curricular campus organization supported by Loyola University Maryland's Office of Student Activities.

Eclectic and provocative, Apprentice House titles intend to entertain as well as spark dialogue on a variety of topics. Financial contributions to sustain the press's work are welcomed. Contributions are tax deductible to the fullest extent allowed by the IRS.

To learn more about Apprentice House books or to obtain submission guidelines, please visit www.apprenticehouse.com.

Apprentice House
Communication Department
Loyola University Maryland
4501 N. Charles Street
Baltimore, MD 21210
Ph: 410-617-5265 • Fax: 410-617-2198
info@apprenticehouse.com • www.apprenticehouse.com